Karl Shapiro

Beyond Criticism

What the Poet Knows

The True Artificer

The Career of the Poem

University of Nebraska Press

unp
UNIVERSITY OF NEBRASKA PRESS

Library of Congress card Number 53-10761

MANUFACTURED IN THE UNITED STATES
OF AMERICA

CONTENTS

The original title of the work which constitutes the Montgomery Lectureship on Contemporary Civilization, 1953, was:

A PRIMER FOR POETS

My thanks are due to Professor Julius Cohen of the College of Law, University of Nebraska, for suggesting the present title.

Man has to realize personality.
Personality is spirit, free spirit
and the link between man and God.
It is a link of man with God which
is outside objectivisation, and outside the false submergence of man in
his own closed circle. Through it
is revealed infinity and eternity and
authentic beauty.

Nicholas Berdyaev
Slavery and Freedom

INTRODUCTION

SOMEONE must write a non-partisan (non-philosophical, non-scientific, non-mystical) book about poetry, a book that steers between the extremes of objectivity and intuition, a book that avoids theories of value as well as the mechanics of structure, a book that takes poetry for itself and not as a substitute for something else, a book that keeps poetry on a plane with other kinds of knowledge, neither above nor below them, a book that has no desire to further a cause and no desire to destroy one, a book without cultural hysteria or cultural frigidity, a book without a single prescription for behavior, without a single doctrine or absolute. What liberating power this work would have! How it would free poets from all the boggy theories of obligation through which they must now struggle—the debilitating discipleships, the social antagonisms, the false dreams of mission and high office and destiny....

The three lectures that follow do not purport to be this book, but only an attempt to establish the idea of such a work. My purpose is merely preliminary: to declare an imaginary truce between the many rival parties which exist in the literary commonwealth. I do not want to set up a new banner with the legend (paraphrasing George Orwell) that all poets are equal, but some are more equal than others. My legend would appear when all banners had vanished, and it would read: All true poems are equal in truth and separate in truth.

The young poet growing up in an age of literary doctrine and counter-doctrine takes it for granted that poetry is just another form of strife in the world. It will never occur to him that he is exempt from service with both the Palefaces and the Redskins, the Philistines and the Highpriests, the Radicals and the Intransigents. Instead, he will be asked to make a lifetime commitment of one or the other fanatacism, the origins of which nobody can remember. Every reader has witnessed a few side-skirmishes of this conflict and can report on its bitterness and its futility. There cannot be a half dozen writers within living memory who have managed to refrain from the Hundred Years War of Culture, nor any who has shown pacific feelings toward all the combatants.

In my literary utopia, however, all artists would not be brethren and bedfellows. On the contrary, they would abide by a colder creed than now exists, one that preaches against the very warmth of friendship and enmity, one that severs art from science and philosophy and religion and society. But what can be the good of such a formula of remoteness? Why have poetry at all if it is to exist only by itself in the freezing outer regions of the mind? What selfish esthetic or private rationalization is this that snatches poetry from the world?

These are not easy questions to deal with, but they are of the highest importance, especially today when poetry is used everywhere as a weapon. Ours is pre-eminently an Age of Culture, and only secondarily an Age of Art. Culture and Art are incompatible; indeed, they are enemies; for Culture is what is done with Art. Culture is the harnessing of Art for power and energy, Culture is the official battle of the world against life. In every country today there are meetings of Culture experts and Culture committees, among them many artists who make a profession of Culture. What are they doing there? In every literary journal we find a symposium on Culture, the attempt to force the artist into an historical role.

If the poet is to be rescued from the world of Culture and the world of History he must first be restored to himself as poet alone. Only then will he be able to view the world as he sees it and not as he is told to see it. By whom is the poet told how to see the world? By critics, by estheticians, by theologians, by historians, and by poets themselves. By professionals, in short; by all writers who regard literature as a means and not an end.

In writing these notes I have found myself falling into the terminology of the military—a bad sign for one who sets out to be a peacemaker. Yet it would be dishonest to pretend that I feel no sense of personal involvement in the literary battles of the age. The pacifist is always in the unenviable position of being the enemy of all combatants; and his hardest task is the preservation of his sweetness of spirit. It is the same with the literary pacifist: both sides agree to get him out of the way in order to resume the fighting; he would be a saint who felt no anger at them.

But it is not a contemporary quarrel I have in mind. Rather it is a quarrel that is at least as old as our country. It was not invented here, however; and we can find similar outbreaks in other ages and whenever the artist has found himself being urged into a position of power. I am going to speak mostly about the contemporary campaign because I am familiar with it, but I will make references to certain of the classical strategies of the past. I hope I have not oversimplified the contemporary scene: I have grouped nearly all the belligerent factions under two standards. One I refer to as Poets of Myth and the other as Poets of History. The mythic poets are those who believe in the transcendental value of art; the historic poets are those who believe in the propagandistic value of art. In order to fix this contest in your minds, I should perhaps give a concrete example of how it works.

A few years ago a literary prize was given to a poet who was in jail awaiting trial for treason. As a result of this award, the literary organs of the country divided (almost along the lines of circulation) over the principle of literary awards. The big magazines said that no traitor should be given what amounted to an official national honor; the little magazines said, in effect, that genius should be so honored, treason or no treason. Although these two positions were really incommensurable, the disagreement spread into attacks on "modern poetry," on obscurantism, on mass culture, and so on. But the issue was more subtle than this.

The object of the controversy was a member of the group I call the historic poets: he was essentially a poet of esthetic-social propaganda, whereas the members of the jury who gave him the prize were almost to a man devotees of the mythic group, who even looked upon the prizewinner with a certain degree of repugnance. The actual meaning of this award was, as far as I know, never analyzed at all, and the resultant fireworks in the literary press were mostly at the level of slander and served no deeper or higher purpose. The losers in the fight were all those people whom we usually group under the name of the Audience: these simply turned their backs and walked another ten years away from poetry.

The bond between the mythic poets and these historic poets was the worship of language, the worship of art. The historic poets had preached power through art; the mythic poets preached the literal sacredness of art. The bitterness between them was a fight over secularism versus sacramentalism, but where the heathen public was concerned, it was thought better to throw the prize to a warrior of Culture than to appease a mob to whom language was only a medium of communication.

It is a mistake to think that there is a struggle between the audience and the poets of Culture, for no audience exists. There are no spectators on a battlefield. The struggle is between artists who want to change the world and those to whom the world it not quite worthy of contemplation.

I am speaking, of course, of official doctrines, and I am not setting about to prove that everybody is out of step but me. One of my chief points will be that good poetry and good art come into being despite the rivalry of leaders of Culture. There is a kind of moral imperative, moreover, which bids writers about art to extend the utmost sympathy toward one's contemporaries: we should give ourselves the benefit of the doubt in these questions. But there is another imperative which bids us to be free from doctrine and convention.

In the 20th century we have set up the convention of the superiority of 20th century art. We begin our study of 20th century poetry with the prologue: Things looked very dark for poetry around the time of Edward VII. . . . The convention of our superiority conceals an official doctrine which outlaws certain kinds of poetry. I have never quite been able to believe that 20th century poetry is as monumental and earth-shaking as the books about it say; and I am quite convinced by now that the official doctrines of art and codes of literary behavior are death to the young talents, as codes and doctrines always are.

In these lectures I have been guided by the hope that I will give courage to a few members of this audience and eventually to a few poets—courage to judge poetry boldly and to pronounce upon it as readers. The war between big and little magazines has only served to scare people off and drive away the birds. Criticism has practically given up its main business of opinion: criticism today is a Greek chorus which speaks for an audience it killed. I shall try to show that all literary dogmas, whether they are dogmas of popularity and simplicity, or doctrines of classicism and complexity, are ruinous to poetry. And if I can only create an atmosphere of neutrality; if I can only suggest a method for avoiding the imaginary and totally unnecessary conflicts of poetics; if I can only provide a psychological device for freeing the poet from the chimeras of cultural war, then I shall have done what I wanted.

WHAT THE POET KNOWS

FOR the sake of argument, let us divide knowledge into four kinds and assume that each kind is free and independent. Let us assume also that all four kinds are equal in value, none being superior to another. This device will keep us from trying to compare poetry with things outside it, as nearly all writers about art have done. Aristotle, for instance, says that poetry is "more philosophical and a higher thing than history," which is only his way of saying that poetry is not quite as good as philosophy. And a contemporary esthetician says that "Art is prayer." One could compile an anthology of sayings about art based upon attempts to compare poetry with other things. Today, we live in a world in which art is considered by some to be a form of mental hygiene, by others to be a form of unorganized religion, and by others to be a form of unofficial philosophy. I prefer to think of art as a kind of knowledge which is neither better nor worse than other kinds, and which cannot be compared with them at all.

The four kinds of knowledge are natural, supernatural, abstract, and poetic. Or we can call them scientific, religious, philosophical, and artistic. Or we can call them rational, mystical, ideal, and creative. The ground between them we can mark off without much dissent.

Rational knowledge is what we think of as science, and it is, of course, the dominant kind of knowledge in our age. I mean to say that we live more according to the rules of science than to the rules of religion or art or philosophy. But science does not dominate poetry in our time. Science has little effect on art for us because of the nature of rational knowledge. This kind of knowledge excludes man from its universe; it will admit an arm or a leg, a circulatory system or a job, an act of violence or a deed of sale, but not the whole man. If rational knowledge did so, it would of course be "useless" and irrational knowledge. Science is wise enough not to invite man into the universe: that would violate the integrity and the meaning of science. There was a time when men would write a philosophic or scientific treatise in verse—but such works contributed neither to science nor philosophy nor poetry. It was when science shook off the forms unnatural to it that it leapt forward out of the Dark Ages into the brilliant light of a true knowledge of its possibilities. In achieving its purity, science put all other forms of knowledge in the shadows and even began to dominate them. The practical arts of economic life, government, and education have become the colonies of science. At a certain point, science has even tried to colonize the "fine" arts and philosophy and religion, but this is beyond its power to do.

The official cultural doctrine of antagonism to science is one of the most shameful aspects of our literature and accounts as much as anything for the cultural doctrine of "exile." The young poet thinks there is nothing in the universe more satanic than neon light; D. H. Lawrence hated wheels; the Henry Miller type of poet has contempt for anything marked "Made in U.S.A." Ninety-nine out of a hundred contemporary poems are aimed at factory windows. But poetry should be neither pro-science nor anti-science: it should neither reject nor "assimilate" the machine (as one poet thought). To take an abstract position about science or about anything else is to deflect art from its purpose.

Nevertheless, there are certain mixed forms of science which are irritants to the artist. These are the social sciences, as they are termed. The scientific historian, for one, is almost a natural foil for the poet. All social scientists, as they are called, seem to be trespassers against art. Social science is reason's apology to man, and these apologies take peculiar forms. One of these is to make a science of man himself. Another is to make a science of man's habits. There is a science of society and a science of culture and, for all I know, even a science of art. A biologist who has collected a million gall wasps is considered competent to collect human beings who have been stung with sexual desire. Economics, psychology, semantics, sociology, all the "sciences" that deal with the whole man are necessarily imperfect. Pure science makes a discovery which can be superseded only by a more inclusive discovery; but social science is always being disrupted by the unpredictability of—people. Most artists and many scholars now look upon the "sciences of people" with suspicion.

Supernatural knowledge, revelation, or whatever you want to call it, does the opposite of natural knowledge for man. It tends to make man all spirit, or spirit trapped in mortal coils until some happier hour. I mean to say that there is no religion of life, so to speak, nor can there be. Poetic knowledge, on the other hand, loves the world more frankly than it loves God, and this creates a natural barrier between poets and holier men. Some poets, to be sure, are men of God and some men of God are poets, but, in general, churches are weak in esthetics and the glory of this life, while most religious poets, so-called, are weak in talent. The reason is not far to seek: the closer one approaches the mystical experience the more the world falls away, the closer the substance of the world comes to annihilation. The mystical is the opposite of the creative process: to the mystic a poem is just as much a "false reality" as any other phenomenon.

Supernatural knowledge, when it is written about, sometimes moves close to philosophy and sometimes close to poetry. This is because of the strange demands religion makes on man: it must deal with the individual life and soul, like poetry; but it must also deal with the absolute, like philosophy. In a time like ours it must even accomodate itself to some extent to scientific knowledge. Religion has the supremely difficult task of relating the individual to the universe and to all time. And its attention to the individual gives religion a great similarity to art.

Abstract knowledge, knowledge of the ideal, is the all-embracing category of knowledge; at any rate, philosophy must take everything into account, and relate all things to principles. The completeness of philosophy is its most famous characteristic: science can ignore religion and art; religion can ignore science and art; poetry can ignore science, religion, and philosophy, if it likes. But philosophy must deal with God and number and beauty, sooner or later, and what is harder for it, must try to put them together. Philosophy touches poetry specifically at esthetics: I have already mentioned two esthetic convictions which have nothing in common. There are thousands of esthetic dogmas which have nothing in common, and we can understand this only if we recognize that any esthetic is only a part of some larger philosophical system. This is not to say that all poetics are wrong or are merely dogmatic abstractions. Nevertheless, there is no one poetics, no one view of art which has satisfied many people for long. Poetics sometimes determines the external character of poetry, as in the convention that a play must take place within a period of twenty-four hours; but these rules do not trouble poetry deeply. Aside from poetics, there is a deeper way in which philosophy affects poetry, and that is, directly. Now and then we find a poet or a group of poets to whom philosophy is a vital form of knowledge. But this happens rarely and we should not think that because there are "philosophical" poets that poetry is philosophical. Nor should we think that because there are "religious" poets that poetry is religious.

The idea that all knowledge must be unified seems to be characteristic of the human mind, and it is a mischievous and even malignant idea. In an age of cultural fanaticism there is a tendency to tear down the barriers between disparate functions of thought: we have the phenomenon of social knowledge as proof. Even in picking up a review of a new work of poetry, one cannot know in advance whether he is going to be treated to a psychological, an historical, a philosophical, or a religious treatise. The same thing occurs in other branches of learning.

For instance, there are educators who draw up lists of books and call them Great; they then extract the ideas from these books and make a list of Great Ideas. Students are then taught these ideas in such a way as to suggest that they are Truth itself. Or, to take a specific example of how one kind of knowledge can contaminate another: I once read the extraordinary statement that the philosopher Descartes had "cut the throat of poetry." This was perhaps a reference to the effect he had on separating thought and feeling, or something of the sort. Now Descartes, whatever else he was responsible for, did not cut the throat of poetry, even in this fine metaphor. A statement of this kind leads us to believe that, at the very least, all poets had read Descartes or somebody else who had read Descartes, and that everybody everywhere believed him. In reality, nothing of this sort ever happens in art, the reason being that poetry has a knowledge of its own kind which does not depend on other kinds of knowledge. There are so many incompatible notions about the nature of poetry that it would take an encyclopedia to recount them. I do not say this in a spirit of pride, or because I know the true formula, but because, quite obviously, the theories of poetry which disagree with each other cannot all be right. The worst offenders in this realm are the philosophers and the poets themselves.

Of the many false paths which poetry can take, because of its attraction to other forms of knowledge, there are three which are the most conspicuous. One is toward classicism, formalism, and myth. In this category we find most poetry which is symbolic and metaphysical; and such poetry eventually turns into philosophy or religion. The second false path is toward public speech, rhetoric and history. In this category, we find most of the poetry and art which advocates human progress and discourses on man's fate. The third category is toward self-regard, ego, and sentimentality, but as this kind of art usually represents no more than failure of talent, we shall not discuss it at all.

Mythic poetry and historic poetry are the two banners under which most modern literati today range themselves, and most of my remarks will be concerned with their habits, their desires, and their manner of waging war. Specifically, I want to deal with these general faults of poetic theory and practice: the idea of poetry as something that has happened to prose; the idea of poetry as a figment of the imagination; poetry as transcendental knowledge and religion; poetry as history. In the last two categories (which I shall devote the most space to) there is the common factor of language-worship. Language-worshippers sometimes cross the line from myth to history and back again. The fight between them is a fight for power.

Literary theorists have nearly always thought of poetry as some kind of transformation of prose. If they have not found it to be prose transformed, they have found it to be an inspired code, the voice of hidden oracles, the gods, the buried consciousness of man or some such mystery. Between the artisan poet and the oracular poet there are many fixed theories, but these two represent the extreme positions. And yet poetry does not come out of "embellishment" (a term without meaning in art) nor does it come out of trance, as mystic knowledge is supposed to do. In order to give poetry meaning, philosophers and critics have had to say that poetry it at bottom the voice of the gods, or the voice of all men or that it pertains to the conscience of all men or to the nature of all men; they have had to say that it is either imitation or expression. The desire to make poetry "universal" is apparently irrepressible: equally irrepressible is the idea that the poet is a trumpet through which sound all the rumblings of Hell and the suspirations of Paradise. And the most rationalistic theory of poetry says that it is only somebody else's best thoughts put into memorable snippets of song.

We are always taught that poets get their ideas and plots from other people, and that they then put these ideas and plots into poetry. Poetry is something that holds ideas and the container is called Form. It seems perfectly sensible to look at it that way, and many critics are content to let it go at that. But this view is just about as meaningful as the description of man as a spirit encased in flesh.

A slightly more sophisticated school of pedagogy teaches that poetry is not a casing that holds ideas but a kind of stomach in which the ideas are digested and transformed. This is a much more diplomatic approach to poetry and is one that even contains some truth. In any case, it could hardly offend anyone, except poets. Critics are constantly studying poets to find out how they have digested their reading, and this probing drives some poets to look for books that practically nobody has heard of. One poet once wrote a young poetess that by the time she was forty she would thank God to find a book she hadn't yet read. This is odd advice, considering that poetry existed before books and even before writing. Poetry is bound to be something more than warmed-over philosophies, uncopyrighted plays, and misinterpreted history. It is indeed.

The most orthodox idea about poetic knowledge, the one we are usually taught (by inference) in school, is that it doesn't exist. When we begin to *study* poetry—for it is assumed that poetry is a dialect—we are soon led to the books which our poet read in his college. We track down the source of "trailing clouds of glory," and that is that.

Most poetry does not seem to offer much poetic knowledge of a primary kind: it does not deal with an obvious metamorphosis in the poet's life; and this fact gives aid and comfort to the people who think poetry is unoriginal. For every poem that presents an original character, like Caliban, or an original philosophic idea, there are a thousand, just as good, which seem to repeat a character or idea. These poems, however, are concerned with the personal conflict between the poet and "common" knowledge. The knowledge may be out of mythology or out of the almanac; it can come from any source. The contribution to poetic knowledge here consists of the conflict itself and the degree to which the poet has been changed by this type of intellectual experience. The plot or the character may or may not be changed: that is incidental. The poet and consequently the poem must show metamorphosis: that is what is crucial.

Shakespeare gives Polonius, whom he calls a fool, much rational poetry to say: "neither a borrower nor a lender be," "be thou familiar but by no means vulgar," and even the noble γνῶθί σεαυτόν, "to thine ownself be true." Then he has him killed. We cannot expect anything of polonian knowledge except the universal. And of course rational people seize on the poetry of maxims to show that poetry is "natural" and that it has a basis in common experience. *But there is no basis of common experience in art except the work of art itself.* Far from diminishing the value and the wonder of art, this dictum seems to me to raise art to a place of eminence among the works of man.

Another misleading theory about poetic knowledge is that it is imaginative knowledge, and this idea has been greatly abused by poets as well as critics. A century ago certain poets tried to limit the meaning of the term *imagination* but only succeeded in making it a synonym for what we call the creative process. I am no philologist, but I think the mix-up over the term *imagination* comes from its connection with the word *image*. The poet makes images, poetry is image-knowledge, but it is not imaginative knowledge. The imagination is the fool in the house, says a mystic, and it is so with poetry. Poetic knowledge is not a leaping to the unknown; on the contrary, it is a painful engagement with the known. In poetry the imagination can produce pleasure domes, but more often the imagination works like a toy-factory which turns out toy and sometimes real monsters. Imagination can only yield intuitions, some of which are true and some not. Intuitive poetry is just as unreliable as intuitive science. Theories of the imagination usually come from very quixotic poets who are really in love with progress and destiny. It seems to me that imagination is more the property of inventors like Thomas Edison than of poets like Shakespeare. Shakespeare himself poked fun at the imagination which makes weasels of clouds and bushes of bears; he used the term otherwise to mean the image-making and name-giving genius of poets.

There is one development of recent art—it happened sporadically in the past—which is a true form of imaginative art; it is called surrealism. Surrealism tries to break down all barriers between the subject and the object and to produce a delirium of reality. But this delirium is as artificial as an invented dream, lacking both spontaneity and selectivity. Surrealism is one of the more advanced forms of public speech and it is popular with the poet who is most interested in translating dogma into sensation.

Next, there is the idea of poetry as transcendental knowledge. At present, the two chief schools of poetry are the ones called metaphysical and symbolist. In point of fact, they are not very important in terms of production, but they are the most talked about. Indirectly they have had a small (local) effect on poetry and a large effect on poetics. But in general all the discussion we hear about them only obscures the fact that there is more discussion than poetry. Metaphysical poetry is said to be concerned with myth, and myth in modern terminology does not mean a belief that no one any longer believes in: it means a belief that people would like to belive in, if they knew what to believe. Hence, to say that you don't care about myth is, to a lover of the metaphysical school, as bad as saying that the universe doesn't exist. Not to believe in myth is even more serious than not believing in Original Sin, because without myth there could be no Original Sin in the first place. Any discussion of metaphysical poetry is bound to be academic, however, because there is almost no such poetry today. A few poets have tried to imitate John Donne and George Herbert, but without much luck. On the other hand, there are poets whose experience of life is largely philosophical, in a real and literal sense, and some of these even talk about metaphysics in their poetry. But that is quite another kettle of fish from writing a poem, say, like *The Ecstasy*. Metaphysical poetry is also concerned with scientific method of a peculiar homemade variety. It looks for formulas to explain extra-physical sensation (as in Donne's poem); it uses the vocabulary of mechanics; and it imitates the inorganic rather than the organic in life. "Metascientific" would be a more accurate term for this kind of poetry, for "metaphysical" poetry seldom progresses beyond popular science.

Symbolist poetry, however, does exist, although it is "officially" dead. The French have been trying to pin symbolism on Poe for a hundred years, and they may succeed yet, but symbolism is something that will always be associated with the country of its origin.

The poet Mallarmé describing a bicyclist once said that he is "one who unwinds between his legs the image of an endless rail." He did not say this in a poem but in a poetry notebook; nevertheless it is the kind of poetic knowledge that interested the symbolists. The curious thing about this sort of knowledge is that it is neither poetic nor rational nor religious nor even mythic knowledge. It is knowledge arrived at by that amazing faculty of the mind which we call the sense of humor. I would describe symbolist knowledge as poetic humor which is not funny. Nothing, in fact, could be more serious, for the symbolist searches for the higher reality beyond words and beyond ideas. The quality of Mallarmé's statement is complex: it is brilliant, precise, and senseless. I do not know what true poetic knowledge about a cyclist would be– that would depend on the poet–but this example of Mallarmé's comes pretty close to abstract knowledge. Many symbolists, of course, end up as amateur philosophers, causing such poets as Wallace Stevens (the most French of American poets) to mutter abjectly that poetry is only a kind of unofficial philosophy. Symbolist poets tried to get as far away from literal meaning as possible, in theory at least, and at other times tried to collect every possible meaning of a word into one usage. When James Joyce says *shaving-mug,* you have to think of the Great Chalice of Antioch, female fertility, and lilies-of-the-valley. The symbolists ran so far from what they called Rhetoric that the very mention of ideas sent them scuttling. This attitude has been taken as a justification for poetry in which the arts of persuasion are taboo. But even a symbolist work is "rhetorical" to the extent that it persuades the reader of its credibility; and any poem goes bad that leaves credibility for argumentation, generalization, and abstraction.—I am not attempting to define symbolism and metaphysical art, as you see, but only to make a comment about the kind of knowledge these schools are concerned with.

One of the results of symbolist and metaphysical poetry has been to encourage a religion of language. Every poet loves language almost more than anything else, but this is not the same thing as adoration of language. Modern poets and critics have the two things so mixed up with each other and with the mystical Logos that one despairs of ever seeing a clear statement on the subject. The adoration of language is of course a "myth" in the sense that modern critics use the word—they say that language is sacrosanct. Now it may be true that language is sacrosanct, but we can respect this belief only in the way in which we respect the savage's belief in amulets. The mischief, however, comes with those poets who pin the destiny of the world on the state of the language. It was Mallarmé who raised the battlecry about purifying the dialect of the tribe—an odd thing for an anti-rhetoric man to do, unless he was being funny. And this was done in an elegiac poem about Poe, of all people. Whatever else Poe did, he certainly did not purify the dialect of the American, or any other tribe. Be that as it may, this purification ceremony takes a lot of time and energy of living poets: they talk about the debased state of language, mass language, official language, and so on, as if they were members of an Inquisition or of a Health Department. Certainly there are forms of language which are debased, but I do not see why this should worry the poet any more or less than it does the corner policeman. But the point is that the myth of language is one of those false messiahs which many people take seriously and even mistake for the meaning of poetry. Such a high-sounding doctrine approaches being a religion: I bring it up for that reason. A religion of language is degrading to art, when it is not simply absurd. Poetic knowledge can sometimes be located completely in love of language, but such a poetry will be a special and self-limiting variety. To make language the be-all and the end-all of poetry, and not only poetry, but life itself, even symbolically, is a form of literary madness. Language worship is widespread today; the one acceptable "mythic" plot for the modern poet seems to be the Death of Language and the Rebirth of the Word. Mighty libraries are being written about this piece of solemn nonsense.

Language-worship in one form takes the road to transcendental knowledge, religion, or philosophy. In the terminology of modern criticism, the kind of poet who takes this path is called Major, because of his influence on other people's ideas through what are termed myths. But there is an even more prevalent form of Language-worship, which takes the road to History, and its standard-bearers are called Great. "Great" in this meaning of the word refers to generalship in art and the politics of art. The Great poet may cross the line to the field of myth and come back again—in fact, there is considerable traffic in arms behind the scene of battle.

The poet of public pretensions, the poet of history, is the one who is also known as the experimenter, the innovator, the revolutionary. It is my intention here to avoid naming names unless I can mention them favorably or at least with neutrality; but I feel obliged, for the sake of clarity, to give at least one example of the artist of history. I choose as my example the painter Picasso, in the belief that things said about one art are true of the other arts.

The artist like Picasso declares war on the world and especially on the world of his medium; that is, he is nihilistic even about language. Having no real center in love, no rooted attachment to his situation, the revolutionary artist tries conquest after conquest, each more daring and destructive than the last. Many of the works of such an artist are themselves without center, violent, empty, destructive, sentimental. He converts everything into his version of it—a war, the organs of the body, the periods of art, statistics, the gods. In most cases this kind of artist develops intransigent political or religious views which would impose a new order of life on mankind. For the worshipper of language, it is only one step from the slogan "Remake the Language" to "Remake the World." Other innovators are finalists, so to speak, who dream of creating the novel to end all novels, or the last poem. The spirit of competition is heavy among them.

We must not oversimplify the behavior of the historic poet and expect him to be a noted Fascist or Communist like Pound or Picasso. Often the historic poet is a democrat and a libertarian: the basis of similarity between them is in adoration of art and the use of language as an instrument of power. Most poets in the modern anthology are language-worshippers of the historic rather than the mythic persuasion. Many of them give the impression of tremendous objectivity and even saintliness in their lives and work. But nearly all of them believe in the redemption of the world through art.

I have mentioned four misleading theories of poetry: poetry as a form of prose, poetry as imagination, poetry as myth, and poetry as history. It remains now to describe what I believe true poetry to be.

II

Someone has said that poetry is everywhere at its goal. That is so. Many of the disagreements of critics throughout history over what poetry is results from their approach to poetry. Most critics come to poetry with a split consciousness: they are as interested in the cause of the poem (which they call its meaning) as they are in the poem itself, or they are interested in the poem's effect on history, or they are interested in the mechanics of the poem and will not approach it until they have put on the white overalls of analytical criticism.

To say that poetry is everywhere at its goal is to say that poetry gives us knowledge of its own kind, a unique, unrepeatable, intelligible form. Poetic knowledge is neither intuitive, nor provable, nor ordered, nor consistent, but self-contradictory, beyond demonstration, beyond proof. We accept it by conviction or not at all. We accept it as we accept the belief in another's pain or pleasure, or we reject it as unconvincing, not sincere, or a symptom of disorder. How much bad poetry is only pitiful bravado, a falsetto cry of self-assertion! Poetic truth is in fact personal truth itself, that which comes out of the experience of life, and *only* out of the experience itself. Poetry is not universal, nor is its knowledge; it is not the truth for all, nor the whole truth, nor the real truth, nor the truth in a flash. Above all, it is not the truth of the Outside, of the State, or of Nature, or of God, or of the Cosmos. It is the personal particular human truth which cannot be ordered or reasoned or preconceived. It can only be lived in life and it can only be *made* in art. Poetic knowledge shows no development and cannot be pieced together like rational knowledge, nor even made consistent, like knowledge of the gods. Nor are there any absolutes in poetry, except the absolutes of the particular poet. It is as though there were an infinite number of atomic systems, all mutually contradictory, all provable, all believable. With poetry it is never a question of true and false but only of the credibility of the work. Natural knowledge tells us that the world turns; religion tells us to forgive; poetry tells us that my love is like a red, red rose. Poetry tells us that ripeness is all, and it tells us that nothing is so beautiful as spring (two truths which "contradict" each other). We call a poem a true poem when we do not hesitate to believe it—when it is impossible in its artfulness not to believe it.

Poetic knowledge differs from other knowledge in this also: it does not seek, it does not ask; it affirms. But poetic affirmation is neither for better nor for worse, and we must not be deceived into thinking, as poets sometimes are, that poetry is praise. It is sometimes praise, sometimes damnation, sometimes neither. Almost all youthful poetry does ask the philosophical questions, Who am I? and What am I? But the poet who writes this is still outside poetic knowledge and trying to approach it.

Poetry is innocent, not wise. It does not learn from experience, because each poetic experience is unique. The Madonna is painted a million times by a million hands and is never achieved—or always achieved, depending on whether you take the rational or the poetic view. The assertion is ever new and not a reassertion, not an act of faith but an act of innocence. The poet lives in the eternity of himself and is beyond the reach of worldly historical time or other-worldly eternal time. His knowledge is not of the world, nor of himself, but of himself-as-world. Yet he is far from thinking himself omnipotent. "Oh, I am wonderful!" says the poet. "I cannot tell how my ankles bend, nor whence the cause of my faintest wish." This is sometimes mistaken for egotism, when it is only innocent wonder, innocent happiness. Nor does the true poet feel omniscience; he sees only as much of the world as the soldier sees of the battlefield. If he attempts to see as much as the general he will see nothing and probably be destroyed for his curiosity. Poetic knowledge puts us in the midst of experience; in the midst of particular experience, which is the only kind of experience valid for art. Conceivably, one can experience, say, the brotherhood of man, or so we are led to believe by the historic artist who has the soul and the ambitions of Genghis Khan, but this can only be done by putting personality to the sword and by sowing salt on the land from which personality springs. The question of how to particularize universal experience, such as a social revolution, besets the historic poet and changes him into a mockery of personality. It is imperative for this kind of artist to think in terms of change; it is unbearable to him that there are limits to experience and limits to form. Such a poet becomes a prey to history. In the public poet the historical sense is overpowering; it is his main message. And such poets, when they return to themselves, suffer from the most acute sentimentality: they record the agonized flight from history to self. This becomes typically the music "yearning like a god in pain," the music of repentance, and a hopeless search for something nobler than ego. The true artist, on the other hand, is unconscious of history and never lives in the future or the past; he is pre-eminently the man of the present, the one in whom the convergence of times is possible, but only if he is free in spirit and personality. It does not matter for the artist whether the civilization he lives in is compulsory or voluntary; it matters only that personality and spirit are free to grow. Thus it is that we sometimes have great art under terrible despotisms and sometimes no art under the happiest democracies. One can have liberty, equality, and fraternity and still be a spiritual slave.

I give as two examples of the greatest of true artists in our civilization, Shakespeare and Mozart. In both men ego and time-consciousness are practically non-existent: the personality is practically everything. We do not experience these men in terms of pride or humility or will. We experience them as man, the complete image. In Mozart, who historically is a mass of contradictions—Freemason, Catholic, Romantic, Classicist—we find the eternity of the particular, serenity without voluptuousness, tragedy without self-pity, joy without hysteria, glory without bombast. In him the particular is so vivid, so completely lived, that we enter world after world of pleasure and pain and re-live long stretches of his spiritual life. Through his music we learn his landscape, the preciseness of his vocabulary, the shades of his feeling, the turn of his thought, the people in his view. It is the same with Shakespeare. But with those poets who are trumpets of prophecy, we get everything that belongs outside poetic knowledge—philosophy, rhetoric, politics, and eventually violence in action and social nihilism.

The way in which the poet puts himself in the midst of experience is by poetic sympathy, or what a German poet has called *Einfühlung*. This One-Feeling, or In-Feeling, is very necessary to poetic knowledge but it can easily become an aberration. *Einfühlung* is the utmost sympathy for the Other, and it is rooted in love. But this feeling must be held in check by a sense of probability. The imagination cannot run away with it. When the poet feels that he is experiencing history or the universe, you may be sure he is about to make a fool of himself. The good poet sticks to his real loves, those within the realm of probability. He never tries to hold hands with God or the human race. Religious knowledge can sometimes do this, but extreme religious knowledge is characterized by trance, annihilation, and nirvana. Rational knowledge excludes the subject from the scene and experiences without the experiencer. But the poet includes the scene: it takes place in him: above all, he is involved in it. I have heard that Chinese poetics also excludes the subject, and this may be the reason why certain Chinese poems can be written on a postage stamp: Too little *Einfühlung* leads to the poetry of ego and sentiment. Too much leads to insincerity and the trumpet calls of history and mysticism. But poetic knowledge need not go as far as mystical knowledge and cannot, without violating its nature. Poetic knowledge is not all-inclusive but definitely limited. This does not mean there are certain "subjects" for the poet and certain subjects for the saint and certain subjects for the mathematician. Poetry is not a matter of subject but of presence, the presence of the poet in a given scene. Anything is subject matter for poetry, even philosophy, even history, even the daily news. The question is always whether the poet is poetically involved in that part of the action of the world into which he has wandered.

The true poet lives in a whole world rather than a part world from which he excludes certain varieties of experience. He lives not only with his wide-awake mind but with his deeper memory and with his foreconscious mind of probability. Thus his thinking and his living run counter to the orderly chronological fictions of history and the static eternities of religion. It is this cast of mind too which gives the poet the appearance of madness, and which sometimes drives him mad, and which, in any case, admits to him the company of bedlamites. This is quite a different thing from poetic "divine madness," so-called, and we should not be taken in by the unhappy doctrine that the artist is a lunatic. We cannot imagine madness in Shakespeare or Mozart; we do associate it with the artist who gives himself to myth and history. It is a sad commentary on our world that there is an official doctrine of poetic madness, the reasoned derangement of the senses, and such romantic nonsense. The modern artist who cannot accept the poetic imperative of wholeness of personality moves over into a dream world of nihilism and pseudo-insanity. Pseudo-insanity describes the rationales of most bad modern works of art.

Our modern world is a rational world par excellence and, to be sure, man as personality feels more and more excluded from it. Hence all our talk about loneliness, the artist's talk of exile, the individualist's talk of standardization. This shutting out of man from the world has helped divide poetry into the two hostile camps which I have called historic poetry and mythic poetry. The historic poets try to celebrate the historic state of affairs, or failing that, try to celebrate human nature or the universality of feeling. Mythic poetry does not celebrate the world at all: it prefers to forget this world for an external world, a world beyond the senses.

The true poet does not live in a world of his own, nor an imaginary world, a symbolic world, a transcendental world, a world of ideas, an historical world, or a world in which everything is made of words. The true poet is neither a revolutionary, nor an innovator, nor an experimenter, nor a visionary; he is neither an architect of the greatest thoughts nor the discoverer of unknown realms and new horizons. How many hundreds of things the poet is said to be, none of which he is! And yet he is something quite as wonderful. He is the man to whom everything is a wholeness, the man whose mind and whose senses glow with the wonder of the immediate. And, uniquely—for the poet is not the only man endowed with endless wonder and delight—the poet is the man who must *create* the wholeness of the world he knows. Hence his childlikeness; hence the prevalence of poetry in youth. The poet is in a perpetual state of learning the world; and the poet's learning is by love and wonder, learning by fascination of the beautiful and the ugly, but learning, above all, by making a thing of wonder and wholeness with his own hands. Make it he must: that is the law of his nature, for in creation he creates himself.

This work of self-creation I shall next try to describe.

THE TRUE ARTIFICER

THE mystery of art is the presence of form. The poet arrives at a knowledge of its own kind, a knowledge which we can share, we are led to believe, without form. Herein lie all the disagreements philosophers and critics have ever had about the nature of poetry. For this knowledge cannot be shared, cannot come into being, until it is formed. The world is always on the verge of thinking art trivial because the reasoning mind cannot take form seriously. Form, says the reasoning mind, is bound to be play, and some philosophers at their wits ends throw up their hands and declare that art is only a higher kind of amusement. Why it should be "higher" than bullfighting or quoits then becomes the second hard question. The reasoning mind cannot imagine how serious utterances can really be serious unless they are put directly, that is, in prose.

This attitude about the triviality of form is puzzling because it does not seem to apply to anything except works of art; for all knowledge of any kind is formal, and not simply poetic knowledge. The formality of philosophy resides in logic and dialectic. The formality of natural science resides in the selection and organization of data; mathematicians even go so far as to talk about the formal *beauty* of an equation, thus leading some people to think that mathematicians are as unbalanced as poets. The formality of supernatural knowledge resides in rite, sacrament, and the repetition of formulas. Why, then, is it preposterous for the artist to express himself in form?

Perhaps the answer resides in the paradox that artistic material is made of human experience. Human experience itself is formless, chaotic; at any rate we cannot comprehend the "form" of human experience satisfactorily. Human experience is chaotic, but human experience in art is orderly. The poet discovers an order for his own experience; the expression of this discovery is by definition formal. How can it be otherwise? For he has entered into ties with the world where apparently no ties existed. He has not "sought" form nor "achieved" form nor "invented" form: he has experienced it. He has entered its presence and it exists by virtue of his presence. And when it comes into existence it shows certain characteristics, which are these.

Beauty: a work of art is beautiful. Symmetry and harmony: beauty is symmetrical or partakes of symmetry, and is harmonious or partakes of harmony. Wholeness: beauty must be whole, not fragmentary. Symmetry plus harmony plus wholeness equal formal beauty: that is our equation. And poetic artifice consists of finding the symmetrical, harmonious whole for a given poetic (personal) situation. The natural difficulties of finding such a solution for experience in all its actuality and economy and authenticity make the poet an artisan and the labor of his days painstaking, niggling, and seemingly unworthy of one who is known as a voyant, prophet, singer, idealist, and heaven knows what.

Once we accept the equation of symmetry and harmony and wholeness for art we can proceed rapidly to those uses of symmetry and harmony which are peculiar to each kind of art: in poetry, repetition and melody and rhythmic plot. The rhythm of poetry has to do not only with meters but with melodies (alliteration and rhyme and sound-development) and with the rhythm of ideas and the rhythm of images; more than that, with the rhythm of feeling.

Rhythm is the most obvious and the most profound quality of art. To understand the role of rhythm in art is to understand the very nature of art. To regard rhythm as a secondary characteristic of art is to fall into the hands of the rationalists of art and the people who talk about form and content.

Poetic rhythm can be reduced to meter, and meter can be analyzed minutely (though it seldom is) for its bearing on other elements of symmetry and harmony in the poem. Meter also bears a direct relationship to the language it represents. Eventually any particular language decides on a rhythmic norm—a certain number of syllables to the typical line and a certain distribution of rhythmic values within the line. Seemingly, this is the height of convention and inelasticity, and yet the poet is never at a loss for new ways to vary the formula. The reason is that meter in the abstract has no applicability, while applied meter is as various as the words which make up the line.

Meter in the abstract bears a relation to the language it uses, but meter in the particular bears a relation to and an identity with the sense of the words. Where this is not the case we feel a dislocation of form, and suspicion sets in that something has gone wrong with the poem. The meter in any particular case gives the exact linguistic emphasis the poet is after: thus we do not feel meter separately from meaning; we feel the double weight of the right thing said with the right pressure and the right speed. And this form must also correspond with the poet's own peculiarities of speech, his own vocabulary and grammatical needs. It seems impossible to accomplish all these acrobatics at once, but there is plenty of evidence to prove that it can be done.

The meter of poetry gives it its obvious and visible symmetry, but to think of meter as anything except the symmetry of the sense is to fall at once into the form-content delusion. Meter exists because of the laws of symmetry, harmony and wholeness. The poet is bound to these laws and has no respite from them.

This is the barest possible statement about poetic symmetry. I wish now to touch on the simplest point of harmony, which in poetry is alliteration.

If someone in conversation uses an alliteration, he is likely to be laughed at. This laughter expresses uneasiness, the suspicion of affectation and even of insincerity. The presence of as simple a form as an alliteration indicates art-making, artifice. Perfection in common discourse would make anybody think the speaker had rehearsed his lines: we would wonder what he had up his sleeve. There is also the fact that an alliteration creates a point of tension when it occurs, or a reflection that throws the hearer back to a prior place.

On the other hand, a poet comes upon the idea that everything everywhere is falling through space. No matter where he got the idea, from a Greek philosopher or a Princeton mathematician; he is brought to this idea in his own life by seeing leaves falling from the trees in autumn. The dying season reminds him of human death, the slow death of the world, the universe, etc. Of course, the poet is saddened by so much impending disaster and he is going to try to act this out in the poem. This he does all the way through his work, and I shall take the little line of climax which says—this being a German poem—*Wir alle fallen.* There are two points of harmony here, both alliterative. One comes with the repeat of the *all* sound (which, by the way, runs through the whole poem). Repetition of the same sound is itself an expression of tension and denotes a pitch of emotion. Again it should be said that if one used two such sounds together in prose he would run the risk of ridicule, while in poetry he is obliged to create such harmonies.

The other point of repetition is the lettering, the repeat of the *f* sound. Anyone who thinks alliteration is trivial thinks poetry itself is trivial. Alliteration works in several ways at once: it adds a rhythm to the other rhythms of meter and sense; it heightens feeling in the reader's mind; and more important, it gives finality to the idea by setting it off as a separate figure. In a sense it traps the idea so that it can never again escape. Perhaps this is what people mean when they say that good poetry is memorable. I prefer to say that, in a case like this, the poet has proved what he thought and felt.

All poetry is rhythmic but not all poetry is metered. When it is not metered the poet usually has to supply some other regulating artifice to create symmetry and harmony. Often a non-metrical poetry is highly imagistic, the images bearing the weight of the whole form. In some cases image-making is almost the primary business of the poet and there are poets who can get by almost completely with images. As I mentioned earlier, image-making and imagination are two different things and sometimes opposites. The child who makes a bush of a bear is not making an image; he is making a mistake of imagination. The poet making images does not seek hallucinations but realities, as when Lawrence speaks of the Bavarian gentians "giving off darkness, blue darkness." This "reality," I should add, is not a matter of objective observation but of poetic involvement. It is produced by emotional contact, like the expression we create in someone's eyes by looking into them.

Poetic imagery is not simply picture-making and picture language. Imagery works through all the senses, sometimes separately, sometimes together. But the eye and the ear are the senses most affected, although the sense of touch is probably more at work in poetic imagery than we usually suppose. The poet produces image sensations in very devious ways, and with the aim of breaking through dull usage and exposing the naked sensory quality of his statement. This act in itself comes as close to a description of the poet's artifice as we can get, for the ability to make images out of words presupposes everything else about the poet: his personal involvement with language and with his desire to turn experience into language. It can be said of the poet that he feels in language, and that sometimes feeling does not come alive in him until it has been verbalized. It is difficult for other people to believe in the poet's sense of the physical reality of words; critics try to understand poetry with a more limited sense of language, and this relative insensitivity makes the critic bestow magical powers on the poet. The image-making sense in the poet is really not as futuristic, as "creative," as critics think: it is more the desire to get it right, to say the thing accurately, to find the true value of the locution for each case. Imagery affects everything in a poem except perhaps meter. Indeed, if there is any dichotomy in the whole work of art, it is not form and content, or image and idea, or feeling and statement, but image and meter. Image includes every verbal function in poetry, and meter, of course, is not verbal but temporal. It may be that it is the time element of poetry which, in fact, takes the poem out of flowing chronological time and puts it into a time-world all its own.

The most important class of image is metaphor. This the boldest of language figures and is even a synonym for image. Metaphor takes to itself the properties of all words and is concerned with those properties. Metaphor can assign new properties to words but not with license. In fact, it is the business of metaphor to find out the sensory and ideational possibilities of words which are inherent in them and which they acquire through use and abuse. Only in this way can metaphor bring about the metamorphosis in poetry which the poet needs.

A good image is a good picture, a proper likeness, a physical truth, and a symbolic truth. When the poet calls England a precious stone we get a vision of something small and precious; we get a feeling of indissoluble hardness which resists ages of change; and we get a sense of eminence also, that which is the center of something. The poet then speaks of the sea in contrast. The sea is soft, less precious, fluid, the element in which we find the precious stone. The line reads, "This precious stone set in the silver sea." In metaphorical terms the meaning "beautiful, safe, beloved England" becomes "this land, the king's which he wears forever in his crown."

The difference between a poetic and a rational statement about England is that the latter is more abstract. The historian would say "the power of England." The poet images this power by talking about England as a jewel of the sea. And the artifice of metaphor here consists in finding the symbolic particular for the abstraction.

There is one other element of poetic artifice I wish to mention, this one the most difficult to say anything sensible about. That is the music of poetry. The chief sensory quality of language is music, but the music of language cannot be coded and reduced to scales and harmonic tables. Still there is no question that the sound of words in poetry does most of the work of producing images and sensory meaning. Every language has a melodic system of its own and every poet within his language has a melodic system of his own. And this sound system is based on inherent sensory meanings and inherent verbal meanings.

There are some people who say that no word has inherent meaning, only given meaning. I have even heard of one of these men telling his children that on Monday they would call meat *bread* and bread *meat.* On Tuesday they would call meat *wood,* and on Wednesday *ice.* By Saturday, I imagine, the children would be ready to burn all the family poetry books in the fireplace. On the other hand, a poet like Paul Claudel believes so deeply in the inherent meaning of words that he even argues for the graphic extension of meaning; a word to him even looks like what it means. But let that go. George Saintsbury, a 19th century critic, used to say that inherent meanings in sound do not exist: he was a semanticist of sorts. Saintsbury said that there was nothing somber or lugubrious about the sound of *gloom* or *doom,* as poets contended, for if that were so, how could you account for the word *bloom*?

The rationalist of language believes in the story of the Tower of Babel, namely that more than one language is a curse. Semanticists are always trying to take the curse off words by reducing all languages to one, and one so useful that with it the Hottentot could converse with the biophysicist about the House of Lords. The poet believes in the endless multiplicity of language and dialects and personal styles: he glories in every change the language makes, and he knows that each change comes from a deep necessity in the language and that the language will reject every change which is not a true change. There is a natural French Academy in language which holds court over every nuance and innovation: it may be that this is the assembly in which the poet is the unacknowledged legislator.

Every word in every language is intrinsically and extrinsically meaningful. Every word that comes into existence has the esthetic and moral approval of the people who made it and used it. When we have two words which are supposed to mean the same thing, we may be sure that they mean different things. If there no difference between *flower, flos, fleur, blossom, blume, bloom?* Is it an accident that the word *bloom* may refer to a lump of wrought-iron? Or that the word *love* has residual meanings of pleasure and belief?

The highest compliment we can pay the poet is to say he has "ear." Ear is the ability, the genius, for feeling simultaneously the harmony of the whole poem and the sense of the sound for each particular word. The function of ear is not musical purely and simply: it is the ability to know the musical sense of the line. We can understand this on the elementary plane of onomatopoeia, where sound imitates meaning.

With ear the poet can do almost anything, yet he can never depart from the sound possibilities inherent in a word-form. If a word with a loud sound has a "soft" meaning (for instance, *bough*) the uses of the word in poetry will be quite restricted. The fact that there is always wind where there is a bough increases the loudness of meaning slightly. The quality of the word is limited by this internal sensory conflict. The word *bloom,* because of its heavy sensuous sound, will always cast something of a shadow over the line in which it appears. If the word *bloom* were more important than the word *flower* in English, we would be a different kind of people with perhaps a more tragic, more melodramatic view of nature.

There is a simple proof of the ruling power of sound in poetry, namely, translation. Everyone is familiar with the terrible loss that occurs when a poem is taken out of one language and put into another. Indeed, the loss is practically total. But what is lost is not merely a pleasing and harmonious series of sounds of the original: what is lost is the very meaning of the original poem. A Chinese proverb says that translation is the reverse side of the brocade. Needless to say, the reverse side of the brocade is useless. Translation is practically as useless; we see only a rough design and a maze of horrid knots and loose ends on a dull field. The sound may be no more than color in one sense: in a deeper sense it is everything that creates the meaning of the poem. This does not mean that the sound *corresponds* to the meaning. It means that the sound produces the imagery, that the inherent sensory meanings of the words are revealed by the choice of the word for its context. The poet knows that there can be only one choice for every particular case. After he has turned over hundreds of candidates in his mind, he comes upon the one and only choice. And what can the translator do but recreate the whole poem from the bottom up?

II

To speak of poetic artifice is always risky because the very mention of artifice assumes that it involves a separate and distinct creative act. But no reference can be made to artifice without pointing to particular cases. Artifice does not come into action until poetic knowledge is born. To speak of one without the other is meaningless. For this reason I wish to retrace what I have just said about rhythm, meter, image, metaphor, and ear, this time in terms of what we can call sincerity.

The poet has a dual obligation to sincerity, one to himself and one to the poem. This is a far different matter from the form-content equation. Sincerity to self in art means the power of accepting the reality of one's milieu in terms of oneself. This sounds the simplest and most commonplace of requirements, but it is the most difficult, and in fact the all-but-impossible human requirement. It is this attribute which we associate with saintliness and the utmost wisdom. It is the essence of humility before actuality. But acceptance of the milieu does not mean resignation, surrender, or blind praise. It means belief in existence. It means a break with every other situation, the recognition of the inescapability from the unique situation. It means a divorce from the historical function and a marriage with the poetic-creative function. This attitude is neither revolutionary nor traditionalist; it is impossible for the poet to generalize his condition so far in either direction. Yet in sincerity he breaks through to new land, a symbolically disruptive act which is recognized by conventional minds as dangerous. The true poet makes this breakthrough without ill intention and without malice: the "experimental" poet does it with evil intent. Since the time of Baudelaire the notion that poetry is malicious has become so widespread that poetry boasts of its destructive powers. Modern poetry represents official sincerity, or the myth of sincerity (called integrity), but little modern poetry is sincere except in relation to its myth. That is, modern poetry says that this is a bad world and we will not say anything about it except that it is bad. Anyone who says it is good desecrates the myth. Thus, the approach to the myth of language must be that in this world the language is debased—etcetera, etcetera.

Acceptance of the situation for the poet is the sign of sincerity to self. This acceptance implies less rather than more involvement in the outside situation. The scene is where he is. He does not seek out the scene. Of the poet who goes out into the scene we always ask the question: Is he sincere? The great nationalist poets, the great rhetoricians, the makers and users of systems convince us, if at all, in spite of their giantism. These poets substitute will for sincerity and they carry with them our suspicion that their real aim is to dominate the scene, and not necessarily to know it.

Sincerity to the poem follows naturally from acceptance of the scene. Sincerity to the poem is the expression of the other deeper sincerity. The old aphorism "style is the man" strikes close to what I am saying. It is not that the poet achieves style as a highjumper achieves height, as much as it is that he achieves selfhood and personality. When we say *style* we are apt to think of surfaces, but it is our duty as readers to distinguish between style which is only a mask and style which is the outer form of inner reality. The poet of masks does not fool anyone for long. The true poet is incapable of imitation. We do not think Shakespeare was unoriginal because he used Plutarch and Holinshed. The story is always there, always in existence: it is what the poet experiences from it that is his theme. The leaves are always falling, the ladies are always fickle, the soldiers always dying, the poor always suffering. Some of this sinks into the poet's soul and cheers him or hurts him, and changes his life. And being changed he changes how to say it.

The poet's artifice consists in making his lines conform to the degree of change he has experienced. The alterations he makes time and time again in a single phrase or a single word are not for "effects"; they are a search for the exact degree of change which he has lived and which is part of him. This is sincerity to the situation. But the search for the right word is carried out also in the other direction, in terms of the possibilities of the language. This is sincerity to the poem. Thus it is that all authentic or sincere poetry is new and surprising and all insincere poetry trite. The trite is bound to be untrue because the degree of the situation has not been taken. The trite can only be "universal"; it can have only general statistical truth, not human poetic truth. The term *trite* is also coupled with the term *sentimentality*: both imply half-truth.

Sincerity in terms of rhythm means finding the rhythm of the language itself and finding the personal expression of this collective rhythm. The rhythm of poetry differs radically from language to language, but in one language it never goes very far from a norm. Even in extreme cases in English rhythm, for instance Hopkins, Whitman, and Eliot, who all tried to escape the norm, the basic meter is present. What is astonishing is the infinite variety that exists within the norm of our simple English line. American poets today are making the mightiest effort to turn the wheel of rhythm, and may succeed—but so far we have no proof that a new era has been reached for English rhythm. The most widely used new rhythm is modelled on a tri-syllabic rather than a di-syllabic meter; in Pound it takes an abbreviated form of the classic hexameter:

Surrounded by herds and by cohorts looked on Mt. Taishan

The rhythm is sincere in terms of modern English and it is sincere in terms of the classical aims of the poet. But the form is limiting because it can be sustained in English only by an elaborate use of conjunctions and other connectives:

And the flute lay there by her thigh

....

And then went down to the ship

The whole form spreads because of the meters, requiring the largest possible canvas for work. Modern metrics in general show more tendency to compromise than this.

The poet cannot know what to say until his ear has said it. Up to that point, experience is still in the realm of sensation, locked in. But by being doubly aware of his situation and the condition of the language, the poet does something for the poem and for the language. Language itself seeks form.

There is a kind of poetic soul in language which everyone contributes to and takes from. The poet immerses himself in this language-consciousness; he is at home in this element above all. But his task only begins at this juncture.

Meter is the frame of poetry. It frames not only the whole with symmetry but it frames each part within the larger frame. Without meter, as we know from free verse poets, there is no principle of selection, unless the poet supplies one. Meter drives rhythm into pattern: it does the same with imagery and sound. The lines of force in a poem can be traced through meter: without it everything else is in danger of dislocation. Sincre meter permits natural word order, natural to the language, natural to the poet's language, and natural to the particular poem. Sincere meter permits the flow of feeling through imagery and the sounds of the lines.

A poem must do what it says. This dictum can well sum up the responsiblities of the poet to his craft. If the poem says *I love you* the words must act out this conviction and feeling in such a way as to convince a reader that the act of love is beyond question real. Most poems that fail merely say; they do not do. But the good poet goes to infinite pains to re-create the scene and mood and quality of what he says. Each word is exploited for its image content, and here the poet must concern himself with the sensory possibilities of the words in terms of their truth to the situation and to himself. The situation can be made real only if he finds it in himself to be capable of the experience he is writing about. He searches for meanings in terms of the senses. The intelligence of art is sensory intelligence, the meaning of art is sensory meaning: unless the poet can argue through language colors, language shapes, language sounds, and through the natural image-making genius of language, he fails as a poet.

Through ear we can trace the poet's total sense of harmony, as through meter we can trace the invisible field of force which holds the poem's body in shape. Ear, specifically, is the ability to find the sensuous correspondences of meaning: ear makes physical what is only implicit in meaning. Ear is harmony itself, from one point of view: it is also the guide to sincerity to the poem and sincerity to self. Ear is the critical faculty of the creative mind, but ear cannot function unless the poet is wholly involved in the situation and the situation wholly involved in him. It is an active, not a passive faculty, and it is this which distinguishes it from the faculty of judgment or the faculty of observation. As soon as one speaks of ear he becomes involved in the presentation of the total poem, the wholeness of which is its meaning. Ear, from the poet's point of view, is equivalent to his own total experience of the finished poem: a vision of it. Ear, to the reader, is his acceptance of the poem because it is good.

The artifice of poetry is without science, without philosophy, without religion. You cannot write or understand a poem philosophically, you cannot write or understand a poem religiously, you cannot write or understand a poem scientifically. The uniqueness of a work of art is its primary characteristic. Outside the work of art there is no rationale which can shed light on it. The poet therefore has no obligation to "explain" his poem in other terms, for there is nothing to explain unless something has gone wrong.

Criticism which usually tries to view poetry in the light of other knowledge thus has the double meaning of explanation and negation. But the attempt to make poetry "mean" more than it does is a sign of desperation about other things. Esthetics, I daresay, flourishes in a time of pessimism. Art flourishes at any time when the individual spirit is left free. True poetry does not require explanation, in any case, because of the law of beauty which demands immediate response to the whole work. Good poets never play with meaning: on the contrary they make meaning foolproof. There is no such thing as a good unintelligible work of art. And there is no such thing as a good work of art which is not immediately apprehensible in the senses. This dictum can be tested against Homer and Dante and Shakespeare and a handful of contemporaries: there is always the handle by which the cup is held, be it plot or logic of circumstance, or something else.

The artifice of poetry is essentially dramatic, and no drama is effective without immediate response. The poet is a playwright who dramatizes his experience; he is the actor who acts it out. Most poets, even when their poems fail in immediacy, defend their work by claiming that their poems leap the gap from poet to reader, even when they don't. But there are some poets who believe that the difficulties of understanding are natural to poetry. Such poets are usually amateur philosophers or theologians. Poetic knowledge is at its best profound and manifold, but poetic artifice demands that this knowledge be made to transform the poem into an immediate perceptible whole.

Modern metaphor is sometimes spoken of as a form in which the literal term is buried: the reader has the job of picking the lock. Supposedly, the poetry gains from this extrusion of meaning and the senses are set free to deal with the secondary results of the meanings. But it is quite obvious that the poem loses more than it gains by this method. In any case, such a method throws into jeopardy the entire basis of art. Nearly all contemporary art that goes bad does so as much because of the "suppression of the missing term" as because of lack of talent. To take away from the artist the primary obligation of immediacy is to leave him a prey to intuition and every license of the imagination. Also it permits the theory, used not only by poets but by critics of poetry, that a poem can mean more than it says, and that it can mean several things. A poet who talks about the four, six, eight or ten "levels" of meaning either has his tongue in his cheek or is trying to impress the police. Any such theory is an invitation to bedlam. Every artist by instinct should fight against the principle of multiplicity of meaning: when for some reason he finds it impossible to form his work any other way, he should admit this as failure in himself, and not try to blame the state of civilization, the collapse of culture, the rise of "mass language," and other circumstances which are not properly his business. It is the poet's job to discover the way to integrity of meaning, not his job to destroy integrity of meaning. Poetry that defends fragmentation borders on apocalyptic knowledge and insane knowledge. Poetry that defends the derangement of the senses, synesthesia, associationalism and the like, drifts rapidly towards a religious state of mind in which poetry itself becomes a religion and an art of prophecy. The good poet is known for the limitations he puts upon his material as well as for the wholeness he creates out of it. It is for this reason that the best artists frequently seem to be doing the same thing over and over again. The inferior artist, who abhors limits, becomes napoleonic and thinks all he has to do is turn his face like a bright light on any scene, and the scene will become illuminated.

Poetry creates a total scene only by implication. The scene within the work is whole but it does not signify a system. This kind of knowledge is the opposite of philosophical knowledge, which seeks a whole order. It is the opposite of scientific knowledge which seeks a whole order of a different kind. It is the opposite of religious knowledge, which seeks a total order in its own way. Poetry lies eternally outside any order of things which seeks or finds a self-contained system of ideas or beliefs. The current of poetry continually crosses these other currents in a counter-direction. Yet the liimted personal truth of poetry and art gives the only permanent evidence of human reality we have. This is why philosophers and politicians and even scientists quote poetry: there is nothing else in human knowledge to prove what they are saying. The accurate quotation of poetry is equivalent to a point of evidence.

Artifice itself is proof. It proves to the poet that what happened could happen. The poem brings into physical existence the always dying reality of experience and the bright or blurred sensations of memory. And artifice brings into existence for the reader the reality of the poet's vision. Let us not abuse the word vision: it is an ocular term, not a fortune teller's. It is not the vulgar conception of poetry as ideal knowledge or future knowledge or transcendental knowledge or pure knowledge or any of the things we read about in books of poetics.

The 20th century has made the discovery, among so many others, that poetry must be written. This discovery has not yet led to a revision of poetics: so far it has led only to a mechanistic view of art. We have given up the notion of oracular poetry, poetry of the depths, trance poetry, and so on, but we have swung over to the extreme on the other side.

Nowadays critics talk about structure, tenor, function, texture, using the language of mechanics. They approach poetry through the language of psychology, whereas the vocabulary of emotion among them is considered primitive and even obscene. If a critic pronounces a poem beautiful, everyone hangs his head in shame. Nevertheless, we are better off than the critics who used to talk about inspiration and imagination, and it is even possible that we are coming close to a civilized poetics. The obstacle at present is the existence and even growth of a mythopoeia which would raise poetry to an even higher status than government, ethics or religion. The public has instinctively fought off this religion of poetry, but most of the literary public has been weakened or disaffected by the pretences of mythos. Myth is easily changed into culture propaganda, as was the case in Russia and also in countries where the artist changed to the seer. It makes no difference whether the poetry is supposed to be for the peasants or for the aristocracy: as soon as poetry becomes *for* something or somebody, it is doomed. A poetry that distills values or sets standards or projects myths is at once official poetry. It is tragic for poets and for everyone else that poetry in our time cannot be taken seriously unless it poses as *something like* philosophy or *something like* religion or *something like* science.

And yet the discovery that poetry has to be written is a good sign. This could only have happened in America where there was no poetry until a century ago and people set about (as Americans will) to find out how it is done. We even started schools for this purpose, to the vast amusement of Europeans. The discovery that poetry must be written has unfortunately helped those zealous people who believe in something called Communication. Both historic poets and mythic poets believe that poetry is a kind of higher Morse Code which can be translated into ordinary language if one knows the signals. But poetry does not communicate in this way at all. The poet does not communicate to the poem; nor does the poem communicate to the reader. The very term "communicate" is a propaganda word which expresses a false reality. A poem is a perfectly intelligible thing in itself: it is coherent; it is whole; it is beautiful; but it is not winking at anybody. This is why the poet has a choice about publication itself: it would not necessarily change his poetry if he locked it all in a strongbox. Most poets probably release their work because of a variety of psychological reasons and not because the poem is *for* someone else. Even the common experience of viewing a particular work is, in a sense, fortuitous, for the creator has no obligation to anything but his creation: he knows, of course, that a given work should have a predictable effect on an audience, but he cannot be sure. I do not think the good poet intentionally hides his work, nor does he shout it from the rooftops. He gives it because he is proud to have made it, but it is given to no one. The giving in art consists in the making—when the poet has finished the poem and it lies on the table before him, he has done his supreme act of charity. It would be wicked, if knowing it to be good, he then destroyed it, but the poem says only: This is what I am. When the poet writes a poem "to" his mistress, the dedication can only be an afterthought. The poet has experienced the lady's beauty and his love for her (which is colored by her love for him) but the work of the poem takes place quite apart from this maze of feelings. The poet at the point of creation sits down with the question: What happened to me? Where was I when it happened? His spirit then gives witness of injury or exultation, his memory remakes the scene, he begins the search for words to tell the story. And the *time when* he does these things determines whether they will be done at all. Shelley's glorious image of inspiration as a fading coal tells what happens to the poet who waits. Waiting is death to art. Almost anyone can recover from experience: only the artist can arrest the quality of experience.

At the bottom of every poem lies the personal history of poetic artifice, the ceaseless engagement of the poet with the quality of experience itself, the efforts to reach the poem without violating his own truth or without violating its verbal possibilities. This can only be done by finding the wholeness of the situation itself. Wholeness is achieved through the virtues of symmetry and harmony. And symmetry and harmony in a related and complete work result in a thing of beauty. *Beauty is a quality of poetry and not its aim.* Its aim is to give finality to the particular personal human truth.

There is a legend about the end of the world which pictures a poet standing in the doorway of his lonely cottage, watching the approach of a pestilent cloud. He knows he is the last living man and he knows that death will come to him in a few hours. What does he do? How does he prepare for his own death and the death of the world? He does not sink down in thought or prayer; he does not attempt to record his final hours; he does not seek an escape from the inevitable destiny. He turns back into the house and goes to his writing table; he takes up the poem he is writing and studies it again. He begins the new corrections.

This is the legend of the true artificer.

THE CAREER OF THE POEM

A DELICIOUS obliquity one sometimes hears at literary conferences and such places is the question: Are you a writer or a poet? The question, of course, is a high compliment, if one happens to be a poet. It bestows on the poet the keys to the kingdom; it takes him out of the realm of mere literature and installs him in the empyrean; it frees him from any of the normal ties to the world with which other men are bound; it makes him a kind of god.

There is a part of the world which wants to sanctify the poet and make him an object of worship. For is not the poet incorruptible? Is not his integrity beyond reproach? Is he not a man of wizardly insight and towering intelligence? Is not his learning instinctively deep even when it is not broad? Is he not the sole symbol of freedom in a regimented universe? Is he not impervious to the lust for money, power and position?

Is he not also that Tiresias who sees into the future, who descends to hell and flies up to heaven?

These are hard questions to say no to, but let us say no, for the sake of truth, and then see what there is, if anything, that makes the poet a superior being. For certainly the poet is as corruptible as anybody else, and more times than not displays the manners of a corporal and the morals of a bellboy. His integrity, although he wears it on his sleeve, is very much to be doubted. His insights into anything but poetry—and very often poetry itself—are apt to be as wrong as anyone else's: we have only to think of the political writings of poets. His intelligence varies as much as that of other men and bears only an indirect relationship to his talent. His learning is always suspect. His love of physical freedom is another superstition: many poets would be perfectly happy in jail if they didn't have to work. As for freedom from money-lust, power or position, one has only to read the lives of the poets to be disabused of this fantasy. A history of literary politics would read like a combined version of the more lurid pages of Gibbon and the Marquis de Sade.

Poetic fame, poetic honor, or what you will, is part of the iconography of history. The fame of Byron on the Continent had nothing to do with his poetic stature and everything to do with his role of hero. Being a poet helped his heroics; the heroics did not always improve his poetry. History seizes on the heroic element in the artist and hugs it for dear life. And sometimes the artist himself adopts this quixotic pose, and he then becomes a party to a literary conspiracy and begins to confuse poetry with history, logic, science, system-making and God.

Nevertheless, the world wants the poet for what he is not, and the foolish poet goes to the world. This liaison results in the two false uses of art which we have been discussing: the one that makes the poet a man of the people, or a man who leads people, or a man who makes the whole world kin, or a man who states universal truths. This is the idea of the historic poet. And the other that makes the poet a purveyor of myths, an oracle, a seer, an almost-philosopher, an aristocrat of the spirit, a being who perceives transcendental relationships. This is the idea of the mythic poet.

Literature of this kind always produces doctrines and fiats and manifestoes. After a time it becomes anathema for the historic poet to write anything which is not a folksong, a patriotic ballad, a rhetorical screed, an epic, or a Methodist hymn. In the other camp it becomes anathema to write anything which does not add to a symbolic system of ideas, or which does not code or decode the mythos of culture. Perceiving this strife, the readers of poems, if there are any left, decide that it is a fight between pessimists and optimists, intellectuals and emotionalists, romantics and classicists, or some other misleading dualism.

Now and then we get a really consistent poet who will align his politics, his religion, his science, and his philosophy so that they all work together. As I pointed out earlier, we then have what is called a Great poet. Even if in the nature of his system this poet must decide to eliminate people themselves, he is still called Great. The term refers to a kind of military genius. On the other side, we have the poet who perpetuates myths of the ideal world or the dream world, and this one is called a Major poet. Yeats is Major but not Great. Pound is Great but not Major. A minor poet, incidentally, is one who has no master plan of strategy either for the world or for the cosmos. Rilke, who is probably the best modern poet, is neither major nor minor nor great and is something of an embarrassment to critics. He is both emotional and "intellectual," both obscure and simple, both metaphysical and symbolist, both formalist and anti-traditional: in short, he is himself, like any poet who abdicates from theory and literary politics.

Both historic and mythic poets regard themselves as official poets. They acquire aides-de-camp among the estheticians and the press, and conduct their affairs along the lines of any other business or political enterprise.

The desire of these official poets to provide answers to all questions is indicative of the intellectual temper of the times we live in, and is not confined to artists, by any means. A man who makes a discovery about the mind develops a psychology to explain all human behavior. An historian will explain all history by means of a theory of cycles. An economist will retell the story of man from the point of view of physical want. One man will explain everything about the human race from the dogma of the Fall of Man. A later prophet will see all history as a noble struggle to improve—the dogma of the Rise of Man.

Literature is contaminated by systems. The libertarian poet, the religious poet who plies the dogma of his church, even the "scientific" metaphysical poet: these look for an absolute doctrine of life on which to build. In a healthy world this slavery to ideas does not exist and the members of my quadrivium do not contaminate each other. Philosophy pursues the absolute and calls itself the love of knowledge. Science pursues demonstrable knowledge and calls itself the love of natural law. Religion pursues goodness and calls itself the love of God. And poetry pursues human personal knowledge and calls itself the love of beauty. With poetry, as with other forms of knowledge, there is no crossing the line, no violation of the nature of the thing, without contamination. All art that does so is marked by insincerity, whether intellectual insincerity (the poet who takes a system of ideas to his bosom and writes verses to hang upon his Tree of Life) or emotional insincerity (the artist who tries to experience history).

What claim, then, has the poet to any knowledge except the personal knowledge of truth or beauty? Absolutely none. What claim has he to be a specialist in culture, morals, politics, religion, philosophy, science or even esthetics? Absolutely none. But if that is the case, what claim has the poet to any fame at all? Is there then no basis for poetic reputation, no reason for exalting poetry among the works of man?

Certainly there is. The seeker after truth and the seeker of truth through beauty are necessary to the world. But they are not rulers of the world or leaders of the world. The idea of the sacred poet is one of the most unsavory and dangerous ideas in our civilization. How and when the sacred poet was born I do not know, but in our own age this superstition has grown steadily for a century and a half. In Mozart's time the composer and performer were seated at table with the valet and the cook. This strikes us as cruel and degrading, but our exaltation of the artist is just as shameful. Perhaps it was when kings began to topple that the artist began the march up the table. This is one of the points of contamination I have been talking about. Those poets who staked out claims on the frontiers of time are the ones I call mythic and historic poets. Their descendants set themselves up as arbiters of history, or of morals, or of standards of taste—practices which have nothing fundamentally to do with poetry. Mythic poetry and historic poetry are both corrupt forms of art, and both are corrupted by power.

A civilization in equilibrium does not make the poet a sacred cow, which when it barges into a citizen's house is hung with garlands of flowers. A civilization in equilibrium needs the poet as much as it needs the priest, the scientist, the scholar and the abstract thinker; he is never made a superior symbol of authority in any way. A civilization without poets is a moribund civilization: it has no love of its way of life. But a civilization in which the artist is worshipped is on the point of suicide. The artist should be treated as the equal of all other people who contribute to the sum total of knowledge, but no more, except within his own guild, when he deserves their honor.

I mentioned earlier that there is no such thing as a subject for poetry; that subject is a matter between the poet and his poem. But if this is so, why rule out myths and the diatribes of historic poets? One reason I have given is that such poetry is false knowledge: the poet cannot possibly have the experience of the whole of the race or nation, any more than anyone else. But another reason is that such poetry is supposed to be sacred, hieratic poetry, and this I consider evil. We should strip the poet of his false honors, false titles and false powers. Of course, if someone were to draw up an *index expurgatorius* of all the mythic and historic poems in history, the world's anthology would weigh a good deal less. But matters are not as bad as all that. Most poets write true poems in spite of their divine mission to purify something or other. Most of Whitman's poems stand among the masterpieces of literature: his pseudo-philosophical-political ramblings we can forgive. Yeats was one of the finest poetic talents of our time, but being caught up in an all-explaining magic, he turned to Madam Blavatsky's metaphysical cookbooks. Even so, he wrote magnificently to his dying day. But why should we allow this license of intelligence to Yeats any more than we would allow it to Millikan or Whitehead? There is no answer.

Poetry springs from the love of personal truth and it results in a thing of beauty. Beauty is a condition of art, an absolute condition, and an instrument of the kind of truth which we are here concerned with. But the worship of beauty is a form of idolatry which is little better than worship of the golden calf. People went to churches during the Renaissance, not to worship the pictures, as we do now, but to worship God; yet we do not question their love of art. Mozart was made a papal knight but he was not canonized. Yet in our time a French scholar has proved the existence of a religion built around the adolescent poet Rimbaud.

There is always the tendency to find some more noble use of art than the mere search for the personal truth of life—as if that were not sufficient. Art must lead others, art must improve others, art must even cure others. Yes, art leads us to perceive truth in beauty. But art is not medicine; art is not pedagogy; art is not jurisprudence; art is not the decalogue. The true poet does not fall into these attitudes of doctor and teacher and priest. He is detached from such quarrels. Other poets in their pride accept the world's challenge and purvey all sorts of real and quack remedies for readers who ask for them.

The apologist for knowledge, and not only poetic knowledge, always takes it on himself to explain how he is really king of the cats. Poetic apologists are plentiful and I will cite only two typical credos. The first was written over a century ago.

> Poetry is indeed something divine. It is at once the centre and circumference of knowledge; it is that which comprehends all science, and that to which all science must be referred. It is at the same time the root and blossom of all other systems of thought . . . what were our aspirations . . . if poetry did not ascend to bring light and fire from those eternal regions where the owl-winged faculty of calculation dare not ever soar? . . .

These wild sayings need no comment except this: Shelley redeems them, and all but refutes them, in the same essay. And yet it is precisely the hysteria of apologists which we must guard against. I quote next from an essay written only a few years ago by a man whose object is to justify to the world the ways of modern poets. This is typically the contemporary position about the value of poetry.

> It seems likely that one reason there has been so little great literature is that at most times so little has been required of it: how often has a Virgil felt obligated to create the myth of imperial culture? . . . how often has a Dante turned up to put into actual order all that had been running into the disorder of the rigid intellect and the arbitary will? Ordinarily, past times have required little of literature in the way either of creating or ordering a culture. The artist's task was principally to express the continuity of his culture and the turbulence that underlay it. . . . Those who seem to be the chief writers of our time have found their subjects in attempting to dramatize at once both the culture and the turbulence it was meant to control,

> and in doing so they have had practically to create . . . the terms, the very symbolic substance, of the culture as they went along. . . .

It is not easy to understand this excerpt from Mr. Blackmur, chiefly because it is so loaded with pseudo-scientific jargon, but in essence it does not differ from Shelley. Or rather, it is Shelley with the interposition of modern science midway and Matthew Arnold three quarters of the way. And it is a retreat from Shelley in that it concedes the abdication of the poet-king: the king of knowledge is now in a university library brooding over the usurpation.

The true poet is a constant prey to the world and its leaders because of his inability to accept knowledge he has not tested for himself. This almost scientific intransigence makes him both untouchable and desirable. He is fair game for the world's rulers and is as subject to kidnaping as those physicists who end up in a closed city built for the dreams of science. Hence the poet sometimes becomes the tool of the objective thinkers of the world and betrays his nature and purpose by trying to make his truth available to others. That, in fact, is the antinomy in poetic knowledge; that the artist is restricted to his own world and cannot universalize what he knows. He can do no more than find the form of what he knows and relive himself through creativity. Thus poetry is neither historic nor prophetic but occupies a separate world of time and value. The implication that the poet is a spiritual brother of God, both being members of the same profession, is intolerable. The poet cannot even enjoy as much spiritual intimacy with God as the mystic or the saint, nor can his knowledge of God be as intelligible as that of the metaphysician. The poet's spiritual rapport with God is relatively crude and is like that of the magician and the psychologist rather than that of the mystic. For the poet, the unitive experience is forever blocked by the nature of creative work, art being an embodiment of personality and not a surrender of personality to the larger Being.

But poetry is not solipsistic knowledge, nor is it knowledge of the infinite, nor even of the distant. Poetry is knowledge of the self only, but there is no self without a world, and no embodiment of self without art. To extend the poet's meaning beyond this point is to render him and his work meaningless. This is what usually happens when we touch art with the wand of doctrine.

History, I have already said, is a precious and noble fiction. Without it we would be living in a temporal chaos. Only saints can live without history. History indeed is the vital core of civilization: it gives us the symbology of our lives. History might even be called the world's poem, the poem by all hands, because history does for the world what the poet does for himself: it creates its image. But the poet himself, the true poet, must live outside history like the saint. This is self-evident: if he accepts history he will be silent to the truth in himself.

The fate of works of art is always a matter of chance. The history of art is a history of chance. The historian of art, to be convincing, must be as much artist as historian, for history, like all other knowledge, must be formal and exclusive. The hierarchy of values is also a fiction, and is always being upset by new turns of history and by the advent of new works of art. For this reason, no good historian attempts to write history while it is happening, any more than a poet tries to write a poem while he is making love.

The French symbolists attempted to evaluate poetry by evolving a sempiternal time-formula for the work of art. The poet was conceived as body, the poem as soul. It was indeed a perversion of the old Manichaeist theory in which the world was considered evil. The symbolist was a potential suicide who spent his holidays in the cemetery; he was the author of the clever and infamous doctrine that the poem begins to live when the poet is lain in the tomb. And it was this flattering unction that gave the blessing to all future "purists" in art.

Poetic reputation, like the career of a work of art, cannot be understood in terms of value. Poetic reputation has to do with the fact that value is attributed to a particular piece of work. There are so many examples of this in the history of art that it is difficult to find the exceptions. It pleases our historical sense to say that Hopkins was "in advance of" the Victorians and had to wait for the understanding of a later generation. But the *Rubaiyat* had the same career as *The Wreck of the Deutschland*; someone had to pin the label of greatness on it. In one sense, the history of poetry is no more than the history of opinion.

The non-historicity of art is one of its most significant characteristics. For the poet there is no progress, no evolution: for poetry there is no progress, no evolution. There is only the eternal problem of rebirth. Literary historians know this well. A man at the height of his powers may produce his worst work. In art there is a refinement of skill, as in any other trade, but no assurance of success. This fact is true because the poet enters a new and different world with each poem. The other worlds are lost to him and he can re-enter them only like any other reader. This constant re-entry into the world of new relationships makes of the poet neither messiah nor explorer but only a man fully alive in spirit and in body to existence itself.

Poetry intersects with the fiction of history, as it does with philosophy and science and religion. But all this is accidental and unpredictable. True poetry memorializes the scene, the time and place, and the world takes this as tribute. But the poet did not set out to memorialize anything. It is only as a by-product of art that art brings the past to life. There are "periods" of art, no doubt, but they tell us nothing about the individual work or the individual artist. Period does little more than point to the poet's vocabulary. Poetry helps create history: it helps rewrite it. This also is a by-product of the creative act. The history of literature is filled with men who attracted no attention in their lifetime and who did attract it later. It is filled with men who attracted attention in their lifetime and did not attract it after they died. And it is filled with men who attracted attention both during and after their lives, but never steadily, never eternally.

Even the great mythological characters come and go like the lost Pleiad. There is really only one way to perpetuate myth: that is by turning it into belief. But this form of contamination (which exists actively in our period) needs no further comment. The "universality" of a particular myth does no service to art; on the contrary it deadens art. The lively medieval myth of Tristan and Yseult was originally a tale of the triumph of love. In our period it became weakened to a tale of the triumph of death. Which is the right version? Both are "right." But there is a dangerous didacticism in the 19th century version, with its awful wallowing in the sty and its dark message that love and death are one. The original tale is rich with authenticity and credibility: the latter-day version is obviously more concerned with a formula—and a deadly one—directed to history. It is interesting to note that the symbolists worshipped the art of Richard Wagner and saw him as a priest and the opera house as a church. It is equally interesting to note that Wagner himself was a political writer who was one of the advance founders of the Super-Germanic racial myth. The conjunction of myth and history occurs in actuality in Wagner and by implication in the theorists of the symbol.

There is no rationale to success in works of art: anyone who has read the life of one poet knows this. On the other hand, there are certain works which are taken as touchstones of the age in which they appear. Such poems or works of art color the very atmosphere of life for a time. I suppose there are many examples: *Hernani, The Raven,* the painting *The Night Watch,* even Whistler's *Mother.* But these works are not necessarily the best works of the period nor the best works of the author. I am inclined to think that these symbolic works, so-called, are really the brain-childen of History. In any case, they are carried about as standards for a time and are then entered into the chronicles of the age.

There is nevertheless a true fame for the work of art, one which the poet himself values, one which the world values as well. This fame has nothing to do with the esotericism of myth or the power of public appeal. It has to do with authenticity. In art we refer to truth in terms of authenticity: that is the only way we have to get at it. How this authenticity is established by the poet and how it is recognized by the reader we have already touched on. But suffice it to say that if this quality did not exist we would be living in a chaos in which every work of art would be the equal of every other work of art. I have already said many times that this truth is personal truth. It is not universal truth nor is it merely what is called a point of view. It is a truth which the writer does not doubt and which the reader is convinced of in spite of himself; and the means of persuasion is beauty. Probably it is this relationship which makes some writers think of beauty and truth as interchangeable. In any case, in a work of art we as readers can vouch for the beauty. The truth we take on faith. If we doubt its beauty we doubt its truth. One of the worst criticisms we can make about a work of art is to say that it is unconvincing.

The personal truth of works of beauty cannot be equated with mythic truth or universal truth. We do not pretend to believe or not to believe what the poet says in order to follow, appreciate, or love the poem. All we have to believe is that the poet is sincere. Let one shadow of a doubt fall across our minds and the poem disintegrates. But the term *belief* is somewhat misleading; for poetry is more an act of passion than act of thought. Poetry occurs because a "belief" has been kindled by passion and made incandescent. There cannot be a cold poem. And the belief is more often than not a matter of emotion; that is, a belief which pulls the emotions into it. The creator of beauty is engaged in a constant struggle with the reality of his own emotions. Emotions do not exist in a vacuum; they are produced by contact with the world. The poet never moves out of this world of struggle in which his emotions ("beliefs") lock with experience. His recollections of these struggles are the subjects of his poems.

But how does this affect someone else? What is my poem to you? It is an embodiment of myself or part of myself, which would otherwise be lost, as most men's lives are lost to others, except in memory. It is the rescue of my passion from disintegration. The poet wrests from the world the revelation of his personal reality. I need not point out that this is one of the most common themes of poets of all ages. When the sonneteer cries that his poem will make the lady's beauty live forever, he means that her beauty has become part of him; that part which creates his poem. Thus the poet triumphs over formlessness, the formlessness of his own life and of all life, the design of which is hidden from us. For many people, reality does not come into existence except through art. Through art we see with another's eyes, but we see no more than one truth. This truth may be the affirmation of our own reality. Indeed, that would be a lofty enough reason in itself for the high position of art.

The love of beauty, like the love of knowledge and the love of God, may be the metaphysical affirmation of man's divinity. At least, it is deeply satisfying to think so. Personal experience plus obedience to the laws of beauty—those strange laws which every artist discovers for himself—this is the equation for the creative act. And obedience to the laws of beauty implies a belief in the harmony of all things.

The poet's fame and honor are based on his love and knowledge of beauty: he does not love religion, science, or philosophy more, or as much. And it is love of beauty which other men sometimes interpret as love itself. The poet is a man of love. But he differs from others in that he is so fired with the love of beauty that he must create beauty itself. Beauty feeds him with the desire to create beauty. No good poet departs from the obsession with beauty for a second. The moment he does he is lost—off on the journey to historic life or mythhood. If the poet must play priest, philosopher, or politician, he takes care to watch that his poem is not crushed by the burden of preaching, philosophy, or politics.

Looking back on the 20th century, readers will have a difficult time explaining the prevalent attitude of hatred among our artists. But once they separate the conventional myths and attitudes from the poetry, they will find that modern poets behaved in much the way that other poets have. And they will discard the poetry of stereotyped emotions and official intellectual strategies. Culture poetry will find its way to the encyclopedias. The other poetry will remain, more or less, barring the accidents of time.

The poet leaves an actual record of his passion in the presence of world reality. He creates the image of himself, sometimes only a part of himself, sometimes his full self. With Shakespeare we have the whole image; with Baudelaire we have a stylized and fragmentary image. But whole or fragmentary, the image is not always pretty. Yet when it is a good likeness, we recognize it and appreciate its handiwork. And the creation of this image takes place, like any other creation, through love. What the poet loves helps create his poetry and himself.

Let us give up the old pedagogical idea that the effect of poetry on the world is salutary. To believe that men are bettered by poetry is as narrow as to believe that they are worsened by it. Let us think of it another way. Let us think of creation in art as the vocation, and only the vocation of a certain kind of man. Let us then give it the honor of any vocation for knowledge. But let us admit also that the sum total of the creation of an artist can equal only himself.

Such knowledge would seem useless to most men and, in fact, the usual view of poetry is precisely that. What poetry does is to ennoble the man who writes it by developing in him an almost habitual love of beauty. This may be the basis for supposing that poets are better than other people. Perhaps the vocation for art and the occupation with beauty do purify the writer; but this purification can take strange and exotic forms.

The fame due to poetry should not be exaggerated. A poet creates out of the necessity for seeking truth through the medium of beauty. The thing of beauty sets out on a career in the world. Sometimes it becomes legendary: sometimes it fades quickly from the face of the earth. But where it remains it leaves an image of its maker. Seeing it, other men have the sense of one man's affirmation of life, whoever he was, wherever, whenever he lived. Then we recognize, if we can read these works, the intelligence, the talent, the acts of a man who placed love of truth above all things and who could not find truth except in beauty. Thus tragedy and death itself turn beautiful in art.

It may be that everything reaches toward its absolute, the condition in which form can live harmoniously with freedom. The absolute of the poet is not abstract knowledge, not phenomenal knowledge, not knowledge of God, but knowledge of life. Life is the absolute he reaches for. And insofar as he creates himself he has fulfilled his purpose.

The fame of art rises from the world's dream of freedom of spirit. The poet is not the buoyant and volatile singer of visions; on the contrary, he is more the Doubting Thomas who finds it hard to believe in the accepted abstractions, and who must prove them all over again for himself. One might say that the poet's freedom really consists of scepticism. The world admires the poet the more when the world begins to distrust its own laws of conduct. It is in times of disbelief that art is taken most seriously, because then the artist appears to others to be a veritable rock of personality. In such times also the poet is inclined to accept the position of superiority to his fellows.

There is reason enough to exalt poetry. The artist is the only person whose work immortalizes life itself—his life and the lives of those who happen into the picture. It is this work which gives us a true knowledge of the maker, the poet, and of his world. It is knowledge of doubtful value, perhaps, but it is nonetheless true knowledge. One can learn nothing from art, really, except a kind of curious wisdom—the wisdom of love.

I have tried to avoid using specific illustrations and even quotations in these remarks, but I want to point up what I have been saying by citing one poet whose career embodies many of the pitfalls and perplexities I have mentioned. The poet I have in mind has already become legendary in modern literature, and he is generally regarded as a martyr of modern society. I refer to Hart Crane. Crane in the twenty years since his suicide has become the leading poetic symbol for American poets. He has all the qualifications for the hero of modern culture. Crane came from the Middle West, he was poorly educated, he became "urbanized" and an exile from his own world; subsequently he was a drunkard and a masochist. But what is of greater significance, he combined the aspirations of the mythic and the historic poet in one flesh. Crane had neither the background nor the personal stability nor the humility to resist history and myth. As soon as he discovered mythic poetry he made the leap to the world of symbols and its attendant dreams of transcendental knowledge. But he was also a young American who wished to celebrate his nation, and he was pulled as strongly in the other direction, toward history. These were the two forces that tore him apart. What his actual talent was we shall never know, because it is obscured by theory-ridden symbolism, on the one hand, and by quixotic yearnings for the future, on the other. In Crane, myth meets history, and we witness the inevitable collapse of personality which is so characteristic of modern poetry.

What causes this dissolution and violent destruction of personality in modern art, this nihilism which the poet sometimes directs against himself and sometimes against the world? What turns the man of love into a thing of bitterness? Why does almost every title of a modern book of poems contain a negative? What is the significance of our official acceptance of the artist's drunkenness, perversion, crime, insanity and suicide?

I do not know the answers to these terrible questions, but I have tried to suggest one: slavery to doctrines of culture under the guise of history and myth; a slavery to which the young poet is offered no alternative.

The just honor of poetry comes from the admiration of mankind for the creation of one personality or one facet of personality. It is not unlike the honor we pay to the athlete or to the man who achieves wealth or success in his affairs. Our pride in him is the pride of created identity. But there is this difference: the poet who creates out of his life has done so because he was part of a particular place and time, part of a particular milieu and nation, and part of a particular age. The truer, the more authentic his work, the longer will last the soil from which he sprang and the clearer the character of his nation will appear to others. The treason comes with those artists who set out to become a touchstone of their time and place; the treason comes with those minions of culture who try to produce the poet who will represent them before the world. Culture says: We must have Art; let us set about having it. And the mythic poets and the historic poets flock to the banners. Meanwhile there is the true poet who has perhaps never published a line, who lives in a town from which no poet has ever come before, and whose greatest peril lies in his indoctrination with the false mythos of culture heroism.

This mythos inculcates in him the vices of exile as against participation in life; specialization as against wholeness of personality; anxiety and despair as against acceptance of the scene; analysis as against creation. Powerful fanaticisms converge on the newborn poet: one is the fanaticism of symbolism which betrays the poet into thinking that he reaches the absolute and returns to the world to sing about it. A second is the fanaticism of world-creation which deludes the poet into thinking that he, the poet, is the maker of all things. These are the two major causes of false poetry which I have discussed. But there is a third fanaticism which tends to come into existence when the other two have been banished: this is the fanaticism of ego which has as its slogan, "All things are nothing to me." Indeed, it is this attitude of the absurdity of things which is today most likely to subvert the new poet and turn him toward some form of philosophical indifference and egotism.

Is it not because of the poet's commitment to total knowledge or his egoistical rejection of all knowledge that there is so little authentic poetry in our world? The artist cannot live by art alone, nor can he live by any of the absolutes of knowledge. He must live among *all* absolutes, however; he must recognize the laws of contradiction; and he must believe in the human imperative of sympathy and the poetic law of *Einfühlung*. Only then will true creation be permitted him. Our poets today are sent out into the world by their writing masters into what they believe to be an enemy civilization and a hostile universe. Little wonder that they behave ever after like soldiers on their first patrol. Little wonder that they all mouth the same stereotypes about our dying world and our dying way of life. Little wonder that the poetry of cultural anthropology and cultural history make up the bulk of the 20th century anthology.

It is hard to imagine how the next true poet will escape all the masters lying in wait to receive him, but that is uniquely and eternally the problem of the young true poet. Nor do I imagine for a moment that he will spring into being filled with love of country and sweetness of mind. We have not yet drunk all the hemlock of the age. And yet I believe the way can be prepared for the next poet by encouraging in him neutrality of mind and charity of feeling; by leading him to those works of art which are the beneficent products of personality, as well as those which are not. And not only to works of art but to works of science and philosophy and mysticism. This job of preparation, almost impossible in an atmosphere of cultural fanaticism, can nevertheless be accomplished if we draw volunteers from the belligerents themselves, and from the long-since dispersed audience. The first step must be to destroy the religion of specialization which relieves scholars and intellectuals of their obligation to evaluate contemporary works of art. Every teacher of literature, every professor of science, should take it on himself to pass judgment on new works of poetry; every serious user of words should do the same. We should respect also the man who is not interested in poetry; he is a man for all that. This reading of new works should be done with good subjective gusto, not with a manual of criticism in hand. It should be done in the first flush of feeling, when the mind is still warm with the pleasure or displeasure of the work. The mortuary gloom which fills most poetry lecture halls resembles nothing so much as a students' operating theatre: the clinical, almost morbid curiosity of the listeners, the attitude of strain, even the applause for the cautery of the bleeding poem, all emphasize the life-and-death grimness of the affair. This is the opposite of a joyous occasion.

The ruling vice in literature today is an absolutism based on one of many doctrines of cultural acceptability, all of which are intent on the unconditional surrender of all others. We should not let the historic poet or critic tell us that he is the defender of social values; we should not let the mythic poet or critic tell us that he is the defender of the Tradition and the true works of the spirit. Instead, we should judge their works, bringing to them all the sympathy and intelligence and training at our command. But as long as we fail to observe our final and supreme obligation as readers, which is to pronounce upon the particular work with our own personal opinions, we give our sanction to the rule of Culture over art. The new poet is always the one who outwits the guardians of the prevalent systems—and mostly because he is not even aware of their existence.

Whatever the value of the poem *sub specie aeternitatis,* it should be given as a fresh, complete, instantaneous thing; for these are the qualities which make for long life in works of art, and even for what we fondly call the immortality of poems. The career of the poem exists only in those moments when the poem is being given and being received.